Getting Through It
A Father's Perspective

– JAMIE ROGERS –

Printed and bound in England by www.printondemand-worldwide.com

http://www.fast-print.net/bookshop

GETTING THROUGH IT: A FATHER'S PERSPECTIVE
Copyright © Jamie Rogers 2016

A catalogue record for this book is available from the British Library

ISBN 978-178456-439-1

First published 2016 by
FASTPRINT PUBLISHING
Peterborough, England.

Contents

Foreword
Elizabeth Hancock, Chief Executive of the Mary
Ann Evans Hospice   5

Introduction
An introduction to the book – Why, Who and How   7

Jamie and Nic
How the loss of Nic led to the creation of Nic's Legacy
and this book   9

Hospice Care – An introduction
What to expect, who they help and how to access them   18

Ian and Cathy   23

Diagnosis
The support network, the hospice and how they can help 31

Andrew and Rachel   33

Palliative Care
What exactly is palliative care?   39

Danny and Emma   41

Carers Support
How the hospice helps carers   45

Jim and Christine   49

Recreational Therapy
Art & music   51

John and Lucy   52

Complementary Therapy
For patients and carers, types and benefits   57

Mark and Sophia   61

Bereavement Service
What happens?   68

Tyler   69

Hospice at Home

   How the service works   71

Other Services   72

What else can a hospice do?

The End

Elizabeth Hancock, Chief Executive of The Mary Ann Evans Hospice

T he Mary Ann Evans Hospice is delighted to support Jamie and this book.

When I first met Jamie, I was inspired by his story and his desire to help others by attempting to alleviate the "burden" of caring, and also being cared for. This book is part of that process with different fathers' telling their stories.

Jamie has also been working closely with his friend, Helen, to develop a registered Social Enterprise – Nic's Legacy - CareNet 365. This has been set up specifically to create a software platform designed to help informal carers and their networks to share the day to day care of someone.

In 2016 the Mary Ann Evans Hospice celebrates its 25th Anniversary of providing community hospice care to the people of Northern Warwickshire and surrounding areas. During this time the Hospice has cared for many people – providing support to them and their families and friends.

When you or someone close to you receives a diagnosis of a life changing illness this can raise a number of emotions from *disbelief, shock, anger, tearfulness* and in some cases, raises the question of *'why me?'*. Hospice philosophy is about caring for the patient and their families in a holistic way and treating every person as an individual whatever their age, faith or culture. Providing care and support throughout their illness to both the patient and their family, whilst respecting their privacy and dignity.

At the Mary Ann Evans Hospice, Our Vision, which runs across all that we do, is that:

"Patients, families and carers in our community experience a journey towards end of life and into bereavement that is supported, comfortable, safe and personalised and is in a place of their choice".

Dame Cecily Saunders, often cited as the founder of the modern hospice movement, said:

"You matter because you are you, and you matter to the end of your life. We will do all we can not only to help you die peacefully, but also to live until you die".

I hope that you find this book useful and should you want to learn more about the work of the Mary Ann Evans Hospice and other hospices please see the following websites:

www.maryannevans.org.uk

www.hospiceuk.org

Elizabeth Hancock
Chief Executive
Mary Ann Evans Hospice

An introduction to why and who we are

As many of you know, the idea for Nic's Legacy came about from me losing my wife to cancer. We knew that something could be done to make coping with that sort of situation just that little easier.

We'll never be able to take away the pain or the loss, but we can make a difference to the daily lives of people living through it, and anything that helps the situation has to be a good thing!

Personally, I was more than grateful for any help offered, but I would never have asked for that help. We see that as quite a fundamental difference between men and women (driving directions anyone?) and how they deal with such situations.

Whilst talking with some of our partners, we had the idea to produce a book. Initial thoughts were for my story, but in all honesty, I keep starting the 'first draft' and then move on to other work. But what about a shortened version? What about using the book to share experiences and memories of other fathers? A book written by fathers for fathers?

Of course, a handful (or two) of fathers that have lost their partner could be a little 'gloomy' to say the least; yes there's bound to be a few tears shed, but there will also be the lighter moments that seem so rare when things are bad – one of my enduring memories from 'back then' is of Tyler - I was belting him into his car seat after a long day at nursery, his face a look of pure angelic inquisitiveness, staring into my eyes, I felt a real bond, right up until the point he rammed his index finger into my right eye with as much force as his little arm could muster!

Back in 2008, Nic only managed one visit to the hospice, we had sorted out the paperwork and were due to return a couple of weeks later, unfortunately, Nic didn't get that far.

My assumption that the hospice was only there for Nic and only for the last moments was wildly inaccurate, although it really was only by chance that I found that out, but it did take me another six years or so before truly understanding the work of a hospice.

A conversation with Elizabeth Hancock from The Mary Ann Evans Hospice regarding our platform was the starting point, not only did she help me understand a little more, but she was also a firm believer in what we are trying to achieve.

So as someone that had received some wonderful and much needed support from a hospice, why didn't I already know exactly what a hospice can offer?

Now working in conjunction with The Mary Ann Evans Hospice, we believe that raising awareness regarding hospice care and the services they provide is a key area to helping people access those services; there is so much more to a hospice than care at the last moment, for both the patient and family.

Along with the very private experiences, we will interleave information on hospice services, just what they can offer and how they can help you, all in 'bite size' bits – we know that if you're going through this sort of experience, you really won't have days spare to read a book.

Some of the stories are from the perspective of the people going through it, others have been written by me after talking it through and taking reams of notes (and recordings).

Please be aware that I haven't changed any of the language of the stories, either that written by the contributor or what I feel are key phrases to the story.

This may mean that there is the occasional word you'll come across that could offend, if it does, I apologise, but as I say, if I feel it key to the moment of the story, then it has to stay.

I'd just like to say a BIG thank you to a number of people and organisations for helping us to get where we are; it has been a long road, at times *very* difficult, but if we can help people going through the kind of experiences written here, then it's all worth it.

Thanks to (in no particular order):

All the contributors – you have made this book!

Elizabeth Hancock, The Mary Ann Evans Hospice
Keith Jeffrey, Coventry University Social Enterprise
The National Lottery
Michael Giddings
Michael Mogan
and of course, my best friend, Helen.

Jamie and Nic

I first met Nic (who over the years also went by Nikki & Nicky) at senior school, although if you're under a certain age, that would be High School. We were actually in the same form group, but this isn't a romantic tale of never being separated from the age of XX, truth be told, we probably exchanged a handful of words in all the years we spent there, all I can really remember about Nic was a pair of white stilettos and denim skirt on a non-uniform day. (And how she loved those white stilettos – well, she was an Essex girl).

I only really got to know Nic a number of years after I'd left school; she was the close friend of my best friend Matt, he suggested that we all go out for a drink one night.

Yeah, like that's really what I want to do; I didn't know her at school, I hadn't even seen her in six years or so, never mind spoken to her, so I was quite sure that I wouldn't miss going out for a drink with them.

Call it fate, boredom, something to do, I reluctantly agreed to meet them both in my local pub – The Royal Oak in Earlsdon (only mentioned because it played such a big part in our life!).

Yes, from that moment, I believed in love at first sight.

She wasn't just beautiful; she drank proper pints of Tetley, she was doing an engineering degree, she was funny, had an interest in bikes (having spent some time with a fella that raced a sidecar) and dare I say it, sexy.

We hit it off instantly, I was absolutely beside myself when the night came to an end, although she had given me her number (landline – no mobiles back then!).

We were inseparable. Spending as much time as we could together and we both knew that this was full on love, we never wanted to be parted, although her university course in Hull saw that we were, at least in term time. Having said that, I would ride up at least twice a week to see her in Hull, she'd occasionally surprise me by just turning up to my flat without warning, it was a beautiful thing.

Jumping forward to 2005, Nic had recently given birth to our son Tyler, and as part of the regular hospital and doctor's visits, we discovered that she had skin cancer on her back. Although it was quite a sizeable patch, the specialist wasn't overly concerned – a minor op under day surgery and it was removed, leaving a sizeable scar.

However, no-one could really say what the chances were of it coming back, it seems as though she was absolutely in the middle of the range they used to gauge it; less than 1 mm thickness and it's unlikely, more than 3 mm thickness and it probably will.

After her op, Nic went for regular check-ups and everything seemed fine; there was no trace of the cancer coming back whatsoever. We were both relieved when the doctors eventually changed the schedule to 6-monthly appointments, it was as though she'd been given the all clear.

In December 2007, Nic went for a smear test, it was quite close to Christmas and we just didn't give it much thought, we didn't expect anything to be abnormal.

The results came back as a problem, but they weren't sure if there had been a mistake with the test or whether something was happening so they needed to run another test.

I'm sure most of you have seen the relevance of Christmas by now; the test was carried out before Christmas but we had to wait for the results until the New Year.

What should have been a wonderful Christmas was turned upside down with worry about the results, neither of us knew anything, although Nic did say that she felt OK.

When the results did finally come back, she got the all clear; it was just a mistake with the last test. To say we were relieved would be an understatement!

Truthfully, none of us know whether that was a warning sign of what was to come or whether it really was just a mistake, but then in late February, Nic came home from work early with double vision, nausea and a headache that incapacitated her – she went straight to bed and stayed there.

Doctors were called and the great catch all phrase of "it's a virus" was bandied about. Nic was bed-bound for pretty much three weeks; a number of visits were made to and by the doctor, but nothing really changed for her.

Eventually, Nic's parents decided that they were going to take her to the hospital and not leave until they had answers. I was working on a racecar in Devon on the day they went.

A message from her dad; they'd been seen, we needed to talk, but not over the phone, could I get back?

The journey back can only be described as 'prison speed'.

A CT scan had revealed that the bastard cancer had come back; spots in her lungs and on the back of her brain.

Even now over eight years later, as I write that sentence, I relive those feelings of that day.

Although I didn't know it at the time, that was the day that my world collapsed; Nic would never have another 'normal' day.

The initial treatment went well and the doctors & nurses were just fantastic, we couldn't have hoped for more.

We saw a marked improvement in Nic; managing to get out of bed, the sickness had stopped and overall, she just seemed a whole lot perkier. However, I do remember one day when she was in bed sleeping, but her breathing was so shallow that there was no discernible movement or sound, for a moment, I did wonder whether I'd lost her then.

With Nic being so poorly, Tyler and I started living our lives through a camera; our first time playing in the snow together, his birthday and just general daily living – at least this way, she could see what was happening.

Nic started on numerous drugs, it was quite a challenge to keep on top of them all; at one point, she was on 46 different tablets each day – some with food, some without, morning, noon and night, it was a constant thing for us both.

It got to the point where the drugs were beginning to outweigh the illness; the Dexamethasone dosage had tripled over the course of the illness, this meant that she could barely move, it was like watching an elderly pensioner with Parkinson's when she walked. To watch your 36-year-old wife degenerate like that is heart breaking. There is *nothing* that you can do to change it.

Aside from a few days here and there, we managed to keep Nic at home throughout the illness, in fact she was at home just hours before she passed on the Sunday morning. No one really knew whether the treatment would be successful, there was a point that Nic was beginning to wonder and she tried to talk to me about 'arrangements'. I couldn't handle that.

I think the shittiest point was after a scan; we went to the hospital full of hope, the Professor ushered Nic into the usual consulting room, and took me to another.

Surely this wasn't going to be good?

The treatment hadn't worked, the swelling had continued, the cancer was still ravaging her body. He spoke to me about the options, saying that he'd offer her further courses of radio and chemo therapies, purely on the understanding that I knew it was for her peace of mind only, they wouldn't change the outcome.

Knowing that the treatment would make her sick without any benefit whatsoever, we decided to stop the treatment (myself and the Professor – Nic never knew). I remember her talking about 'the future' after that point, she wasn't aware that we didn't have one, she didn't know the full extent of what was going to happen.

There were no timescales, no definitive dates that we had to know, it could just happen at any time really. Even knowing that, I couldn't face talking about the situation, aside from anything else, Nic didn't know and I didn't want to change that.

Getting into July, the whole Brown family (Nic's family – Don, Glenys and Phil) and us (Me, Nic and Tyler) had a family holiday together in Anglesey.

Although Nic was extremely bad at this point, we still managed to get her up Snowdon on the light railway. We stopped about halfway up and I picked up two little stones from the mountain side, I still have them as a reminder of our last days together.

We were due to come home on the Friday, but as Nic's health seemed to be getting worse, we decided to head back on the Thursday, at least being home would make things easier, both for her and for me.

It was really at this point that Nic couldn't support her own weight, nor walk, even sitting was an effort and she had to be positioned, getting to the bathroom (which she was determined to do) was a mighty effort for us.

When we arrived home, Nic stumbled through the door and cut her leg open – at this time, her skin was like paper and would just tear, this wasn't helped by the fact that her legs were swollen significantly.

On the Saturday night, she was in a lot of pain, her leg was beginning to turn blue, clearly there was a lack of blood to it.

It must have been about three o'clock in the morning when she asked me to take her to the toilet, my reaction was bad, although looking back at it 8 years later, I know it was only because of the stress and lack of sleep – I'd got into the habit of snatching five minutes here and there, I was living on about two hours of sleep a day.

I managed to get her to the toilet OK, but then couldn't move her after that, she fell on the floor and I couldn't pick her up. I just physically had no strength to do anything. I managed to wake my dad and ask him to come over and help us, we lived about half-an-hour away.

That was a long wait.

Eventually, with the help of my dad, we got Nic to bed but things weren't right; she was in a lot of pain. It didn't matter what drugs I gave to her, the pain was constant.

I didn't know at that time, but Nic had just hours left.

I called an ambulance and we waited – we lived in a rural location and it seemed to take hours for the ambulance to arrive, although it was probably about 45 minutes.

By this stage, I was an old hand at briefing the relevant people; I knew what they needed to know, including the list of medication (I knew it off the top of my head – even now I could recite most of it), so after briefing the paramedic crew they took a look in on Nic and decided that there was only one course of action – straight to hospital. Not knowing what to expect, I followed in the car.

When we arrived at the hospital, they took her straight through to a cubicle where a doctor came to take a look and then he stepped out of the room and motioned me to follow him.

"How long do you think she has left?" was his question to me.

"To be honest, if you told me that this was it, I wouldn't be surprised"

Although half expected, his answer knocked the stuffing out of me; "that's exactly what I am going to tell you. If you have anyone you want here, I suggest you call them now".

Some of that day is still hazed for me, other bits I can recall vividly; Nic full of morphine, not even knowing I was there, our parents arriving, Nic dying in my arms, removing her rings from her fingers, the colour she turned as her heart stopped – all the blood pooling up in her back but the rest of her white.

It took me about two hours to leave the hospital. I couldn't face it.

I still remember arguing with the jobsworth parking attendant about not having change for the ticket machine until a nurse rang him and told him to expect me.

It sounds quite melodramatic, but even now, I know that had we not had Tyler, I would have joined Nic on that Sunday.

The church was packed for her service – one of the biggest turnouts they've seen there apparently. It didn't surprise me; Nic just got on with everyone – young, old, professional or bum – they loved her.

Eight years later …

I still struggle with some issues, I still wonder why it happened; why take someone like Nic, the mother of a three-year-old boy when it could have been a grumpy unsociable sod like me?

Since taking this path to try and help people in a similar situation, I genuinely feel that I have a purpose. If just one person gains a benefit from the work that we are doing, that will mean something to me.

Being a dad has been a whole new world to me; yes, it's true that before Nic died, I'd had a short sharp lesson on being a parent and learning what that involves, but could I really pull it off for the rest of my life? Could I see Tyler through those all-important 'firsts' that would make a parent cry? You know – starting school, starting big school, first proper injury, learning to ride a bike (and motorbike, although rather hypocritical – I'd rather he not have one), being beaten by him for the first time in a video game … all that sort of stuff.

Yeah, I still have first girlfriend (first heartbreak), first pint (first cleaning duty the morning after the night before), first car (first accident) and all of that to get through, but so far, we're doing it.

Everybody says that kids are resilient, they're tough, they can cope with more than you realise, but for me, I reckon my little boy (who's now nearly as tall as I am) has been through his fair share of it.

Over these last eight years, I have always been concerned at just what the lack of a mother figure would do to him. Perhaps that's part of the reason why I made some spectacularly bad choices when it came to my love life – I just wanted him to have some sort of mother figure.

I have no doubt it has had an impact, but I can honestly say that it isn't what I was fearing. Starting at a new school was a big thing for me; we had moved from our village where most of the local mums knew my situation, that involved Tyler having to change school. That involves questions – other parents and the like; "What does your wife do?" "I notice that Tyler only ever comes to school with you – are you separated from his mum?". I used to dread school parties – friendly mums trying to start a conversation with me (which is bloody hard at the best of times to be honest – anyone will tell you that), usually kicking off with the opening line of "And what did she do to get out of coming here then?".

I don't mind the question, I have no issue talking about it, but I know as soon as I start to tell them, their afternoon is ruined; *"What did she do to get out of coming here then?"* "Well, Tyler's mum died of cancer just months after his third birthday. Have a great afternoon".

I almost feel guilty about it.

I think the biggest thing that we've faced is when Tyler started High School. He's always been a little shy, finding it difficult to make new friends. If I'm honest, I suspect I was dreading it more than he was; if I actually *had* sleep on a regular basis, I'd have been having sleepless nights.

He was a little quiet on his first few days, but within the first week I'd had the school on the phone, telling me just what a star he had been in his maths class – standing up in front of the whole class explaining how to work something out (correctly). And from there, the plaudits keep coming; letters and certificates through the post, emails, phone calls and a myriad of 'My Stickers' for good work. Even now, I'm tearful thinking about it.

I suspect that there are quite a few people that would disagree with the way I've brought him up; I'm full of contradictions for a start.

I treat him as more grown up than his age suggests in so many respects – I don't mind him hearing 'fruity' language (but he knows better than to use it), he's allowed to play video games that are designed for older children, he has his own phone and tablet, but … he still holds my hand when we're out in public (although I suspect that really isn't going to happen much longer), we still have bedtime stories and cuddles, he's still called 'my big boy'. I'm sure he's going to read this in a few years and be 'totes uncool' with it.

And to all of you out there that keep posting "There's nothing like a mother's love" type things on social media, yes there is; big old dad love.

Hospice Care – An Introduction

Why do we need an introduction to hospice care? Surely, most people know what a hospice is there for?

Back in 2008 when Nic was first diagnosed, we had our joint introduction to a hospice, just one week before Nic passed away.

Our knowledge was enough to tell us that any introduction to a hospice was a very bad thing, for it meant that she was dying; a hospice is there for people close to death, pure and simple.

It's almost as though the doors only operate in one direction; you'll enter the hospice through the front door, leave through the back.

Having spent eight years working in this arena, I can now tell you that we (see – there's no way I'm taking the blame all on my own!) were so very wrong.

A hospice is so much more than a 'facility', it is a place of love, care, respite, support and help.

Admittedly, I know this from personal experience because I've been through the hospice service, but what of those that have been fortunate enough to not have that need?

There is a high chance that if like me, you've been through that experience, you'll understand just how much a hospice does, what they can offer you, how they care for not just the patient but any care-giver with them.

There is a phrase that seems to be current right now, and it's something along the lines of "enabling people to have a good death".

Of course, in many cases, we don't want to see, have involvement in or be a bystander to any type of death, how can anyone have a good death?

That question is being asked by someone that lost his beloved wife of twelve years, the mother of their three-year-old son; it may be slightly biased, but let's take a step back and see how hospices change the lives of the people they support.

What to expect

Contrary to my rather naïve thoughts, in many cases, a trip to a hospice isn't just one-way. Without getting too morbid, there are of course a number of people that make one final journey to the hospice, that is unfortunately part of the nature of the hospice, but equally, we know that there are also a great deal of people that have an ongoing and long-term relationship with their local hospice.

In most cases, you will have been referred to the hospice through the local health system, this could be your doctor, community nurse, hospital or health worker. As part of the referral process, your medical notes will have been passed along with the referral, there is no need to understand the specifics of the care plan you were under, your detailed medication plans or what happens next; the hospice staff will take the time to talk you through the whys and wherefores, and unlike much of the process leading up to the referral, you won't be made to feel that there is constant time pressure on you to explain or them to make themselves understood.

Whilst that may sound a little negative, it's a fact that doctors, nurses and care workers are under constant time constraints and pressures. It also seems to be one of the most commonly heard discussion points regarding the treatment that people have received up to that point; being made to feel that you need to have any questions or comments ready for the moment that the doctor stops talking, almost ambushing them before they get the chance to leave the room.

Of course, every hospice has their own way of working with routines and procedures, we must also think about what level of care you need; could that affect the introduction?

Who does a hospice help?

Again, there are a few misconceptions that are generally associated with this aspect; I (WE!) were also under the impression that a hospice is there solely for the medical care of the patient, that simply isn't the case.

Not only does a hospice offer more than medical care, but they also offer help and support to the family, friends and caregivers.

From my own perspective, we had met with the hospice just once, about a week or so before Nic passed, although at the time, no-one really knew her passing was so close.

We had agreed with them that Nic would start visiting the hospice after we got back from a week away in Anglesey, but unfortunately, Nic took a turn for the worse whilst we were away – we came home on the Thursday, she passed on the Sunday.

I gave no thought to the hospice until they rang me approximately three weeks after Nic passed, embarrassed, I explained to them how we didn't need them anymore, Nic had already lost the battle.

It was at this point that I began to understand just how hospices work; they invited me in for a 'chat' to 'see if there was anything they could do for me?'.

My immediate reaction was of course there wasn't, Nic was dead. What on earth would I want with a hospice now?

Reluctantly, I went over for a chat and was instantly amazed at … everything.

There was no pressure, no time constraint, no judgement, justification or awkward questions, just an afternoon spent chatting about Nic's death and my ability to cope with it (which I don't mind admitting was *very* poor).

I started attending the hospice every week, alternating with complementary therapies such as Reiki and talking, although at this point, it really was only talking, not counselling.

It became the highlight of my week, something that I really began to look forward to; 6 ½ days a week was torture, the last half a day was my escape. I even found myself drifting off to sleep whilst having Reiki – something that had been eluding me for a number of months. And of course, they understood and it wasn't a problem – the therapist would turn the lights off and let me sleep for as long as my body needed it.

After six months or so, they offered me counselling.

I jumped at the chance.

I didn't know if it would help, whether I was expecting that to be the magic bullet to make things right again or whether I just didn't want to give up my half a day at the hospice. Whatever the reasoning, it helped me enormously, although my counsellor Gaynor was surprised at just how matter of fact I was regarding Nic's passing; I was a firm believer in not looking backwards – that was the path to madness as far as I was concerned – nothing could or would change, no matter how many times I looked back or shed a tear.

Helen (my business partner in Nic's Legacy and best friend) regularly recalls one time when Nic broached the subject of hospice care; "you know, they can help friends too" was her not too subtle way of getting Helen to talk to the hospice.

Of course, supporting me after Nic passed was just one aspect, but for those still in the middle of the situation, a hospice can still offer plenty of support; respite for the carer, medical help, sign-posting to other services and advocacy to name a few.

All this before we even start on the support that they offer a patient.

Of course, we have the acute medical care, but the care they provide can be much simpler than that; a place to just be.

For those that haven't experienced it, being bombarded with visitors and being expected to entertain them (or at least talk to them) while at home can be very draining, and of course, unless you have the hide of a Rhino, it's difficult to tell people that you just want some peace and quiet and hope that they take the hint, rather than sitting there saying "don't mind me, I'll entertain myself".

Access

Accessing the services at your local hospice is usually very straightforward. More often than not, you'll be referred through a third-party, such as the hospital, care-worker, doctor, MacMillan nurse or an organisation involved in healthcare.

In most cases, you shouldn't need to contact a hospice yourself, although of course, if you feel that you *need* to talk to one, they will be able (and happy) to give you all the advice you need.

In the process of researching this book, I've spoken to all manner of people from patients, caregivers, care organisations, surviving partners, doctors and everyone in-between, the general consensus is that a hospice is nothing like being in the health system, and that isn't to put down the NHS, they do a fabulous job with limited time and resource.

The best way that I have heard someone describe a hospice is "It's what you wish the NHS to be like".

In other words, it seems that the medical professionals have the time needed to do their job without extraneous pressure, the staff are trained to be ... human, and where there's a problem, it gets dealt with on a level that seems to be reserved for large American conglomerates; efficiently and courteously.

Ian and Cathy

Cathy & I first met in 2007, we were both training to become Occupational Therapists and we got to know each other whilst attending university in Sheffield; things were just right, we 'clicked' and we knew that we wanted to be together. We were married in 2010 and bought a house together in Oakham, Rutland.

February 2012 saw the birth of our beautiful son Samuel, we were now a family, and were looking forward excitedly to a life together.

I have to say, Cathy was great with Sam, she was the mother who could do it all and do it without breaking into a sweat, she just seemed to instinctively know how to be a mum.

Of course, I'd try and help where I could, but for those first few months, looking after Sam was very much Cathy's domain.

Things started to change around December 2012, Cathy was losing weight and was just generally unwell, we'd assumed that the weight loss was down to 'baby weight' but she went for a blood test which showed that she was anaemic. A history of Crohn's disease seemed to explain the anaemia and measures were taken to improve that. In the time that we were together, I had never seen any symptoms of the Crohn's.

January 2013 meant a part-time return to work after maternity leave but family and friends were still concerned about her health. She seemed to constantly have stomach ache and was still anaemic but it was only when a family member said "you look like a ghost" that we realised more action was needed.

Cathy went to see her doctor again on a Monday morning, the result of which was that she needed a blood transfusion urgently. This was around the middle of March; she never went back to work after that.

A short stay in hospital (just three days) later and everything seemed to be OK, at least for a few weeks. However, a further blood test showed that she was still anaemic and it was around this time that she'd noticed blood in her stools.

Another stay in hospital (this time for nearly two weeks) saw a whole range of tests being carried out, these included a CT scan and a colonoscopy. Cathy was nervous about the CT scan, not for any other reason than "going into the tube" but as with everything else, she took it in her stride.

Unfortunately, the colonoscopy wasn't a great success, partly due to poor preparation, and not much could be seen.

Not long after that, a junior doctor came to see us both and explained that the symptoms that Cathy was showing didn't really fit with Crohn's, they looked to be more bowel cancer related.

As you'd imagine, this was devastating news for us to take in but we were later put at ease by a consultant who stated "no way is this cancer, you're too young, fit and healthy"

What a relief!

Cathy was able to leave the hospital shortly after that, but just three days later, she was taken bad again; awake in the middle of the night, vomiting. So back to hospital we went, and this time, she was put on a liquid diet, the reasoning was that they (the doctors) thought there may be an obstruction in her bowel. Another colonoscopy was done and while we awaited the results, she was allowed home but had to remain on the liquid diet for the time being.

It was about this point that we were really struggling; I was having to look after Sam (when he wasn't in nursery), as Cathy was just too ill to help out. Both sets of grand-parents were visiting on alternate weeks to help us. I was still working full-time, being both Mum and Dad to Sam and trying to care for Cathy, it really was a difficult time.

As it happens, we'd booked a holiday earlier in the year, just a caravan at Great Yarmouth (our first and only holiday as a family) but something for us to look forward to and a break from the daily routine.

We hired a wheelchair for Cathy but even then, she had to spend a great deal of time just resting in the caravan, usually in bed, but we were determined to make the best of it.

Of course none of us really knew just how ill she was at the time. I look back now on those few days with great fondness.

On our return, we had a parents evening at Sam's nursery, we both went and that was pretty much the last 'normal' thing that we did as a family.

Cathy's next appointment with the hospital had been brought forward, the consultant told us in very black & white terms that they'd found a tumour in her bowel but the good news was that they thought it was at an early stage and therefore, quite treatable.

An appointment with a surgeon the following day was very positive, he was open and honest and explained that he intended to remove the entire large bowel and fit a 'stoma' (an opening on the front of your abdomen which is made using surgery. It diverts your faeces into a pouch outside of your body) and with that, it would "all be sorted, job's a goodun".

Cathy was to be allowed home for the weekend, she'd already cottoned on to the fact that if they were going to be removing her large bowel on the Monday, would there be any need to carry on with the ghastly liquid diet over the weekend?

"Eat what you like" was the consultant's answer, so we did – we went home and had pizza! Wonderful.

Again, Cathy woke in the middle of the night to be sick, but by Sunday morning, she was in agonising pain as well.

Sunday was spent resting in bed, she made it through to Sunday night at home, but by this point, she was nearly passing out because of the pain so we called an ambulance and got her back to hospital.

A burst abscess and possible perforated bowel was the diagnosis; she had very nearly died.

Emergency surgery was scheduled with the same surgeon and that really is the point that everything changed, absolutely no going back and no doubts; they found two large tumours which had spread outside of the bowel.

Needless to say I was now off work on compassionate leave.

A stay in intensive care and then back onto the ward for a few weeks meant that although she kept getting infections, she had definitely picked up.

We eventually managed to get Cathy home again and the next step was a meeting with the oncologist and the palliative care consultant to discuss palliative chemotherapy.

The news was devastating; they thought Cathy would have about six months as things stood, and up to two years with chemotherapy, if things went well.

I remember that Cathy was actually sick during the consultation, I don't know if that prompted the doctor to take action, but she suggested that we try and get Cathy into the LOROS hospice in Leicester. The plan was to get her comfortable and get the pain under control – at this point, not even the morphine was doing much for her, it was horrible to see.

We managed to get Cathy into LOROS the next day (Thursday). It was a different world for us both, I really can't speak highly enough of them. We were treated as friends or even family, not just another patient, another 'number' in the system. The difference was remarkable, we were even on first name terms with the doctors and staff, they really couldn't do enough for us. Somebody always had time for us.

I used to work just around the corner from the hospice so I thought I'd take the opportunity to pop in and say hello. There may have been a small ulterior motive as well – I wanted to see if it would be possible to borrow some equipment for when Cathy came home, which we were expecting to be the following week.

Whilst Cathy was ill, I filled the rest of my time with domestic chores and ensuring that all the relevant paperwork was in place; forms for critical illness cover, and even little things like registering for a blue badge. It all had to be done and I think it helped to stop me worrying about the enormity of the situation.

A restless Thursday night drew long into Friday morning, this would see me back at the hospice with Cathy, she was extremely tired, weak and wasn't eating but otherwise seemed OK – I'd arranged to go out on the Friday night with a few friends for a drink, my dad had taken Sam back to theirs and Cathy was telling me that I needed to get going or I'd be late, reluctantly, I left for the night. On reflection, I just couldn't believe how things had changed.

Saturday morning was to be spent doing some shopping and preparing for Cathy to come home. Whilst I was out, the hospice had called to let me know that Cathy was struggling with her breathing, a scan the previous day had shown some fluid on her lungs.

Quite by chance, I bumped into the palliative care consultant on Oakham high street, after a quick chat she decided to ring the hospice to see exactly what was happening. They thought that the fluid build-up was getting worse, they wanted to send Cathy over to the Glenfield hospital for a chest drain.

I rushed straight home, grabbed a few essentials then drove to the hospice as fast as I could.

We were at Glenfield by lunchtime, but I have to say that the service was just… awful when compared to the hospice. I had to persistently ask for morphine. Suddenly Cathy was just another patient on a ward, no one seemed to realise she was terminally ill and in agony!

The Clinical Decisions Unit was quite a depressing place, but we were expecting to be there for a very short time, literally just a chest drain then back to the hospice later in the day.

A raft of tests was organised – blood gas, x-ray and then another CT scan all within a few hours.

After the CT scan the doctors took me into a side room to talk to me: "Sorry, this is it. She has fluid on her lungs and a pulmonary embolism (a blood clot in her lungs), there isn't anything we can do."

Devastation doesn't do it justice; my world was about to fall apart with the news. I knew that it was bad, but never realised just how bad.

It just happened so quick, just like that. The only response that I had was "I need to phone people".

I had two mobile phones with me, neither had much battery or signal, and I was reduced to pacing up and down the ward trying to get hold of people.

I had to call my parents and my brother and Cathy's two sisters. Her parents were on holiday at the time – although we knew Cathy was going into the hospice, none of us knew just how ill she was. One of her sisters arrived about ten minutes before she died, although to be truthful, she was so doped up on morphine that she probably didn't know.

That was 15 June 2013. Just three days after seeing an oncologist who was talking about months, possibly years – a month after the cancer diagnosis, six months after the first symptoms. Cathy was just 35. Sam was 15 months old.

Following on …

People say that bowel cancer is an old person's disease, and while it is far more prevalent in older people, I've subsequently heard many stories of young people with it. It's possible that the Crohn's disease triggered it, although we can't be truly sure.

It felt like we were constantly playing catch up – by the time they found the cancer, it was already advanced. Everything that the doctors tried to do, it seemed as though the cancer was one step ahead.

The days that Cathy had in the hospice were brilliant, I even asked if it was possible to get her back there to die. The doctor agreed but unfortunately, she was just too ill to move.

The whole of the family gathered at mine the next day, I just went into operation mode and got on with stuff.

Monday was spent being practical – registering the death, taking Cathy's mum and dad to view her body at the hospital, just starting the whole process of dealing with a death.

Sam didn't really notice, of course he was very young but he'd been seeing less and less of his mum as the illness had progressed. I'd been caring for him full-time for a while. I remember one occasion when he woke in the night, both myself and Cathy went to sort him. She didn't know what he wanted, but I did. That made her sad.

As I've already mentioned, in the first six months of Sam's life, Cathy did it all. On occasions when I did take care of him, I would be exhausted at the end of the day. Now I take it in my stride.

Immediately after Cathy's death, I was signed off from work, they were fantastic, telling me to only start thinking about work again when I was truly ready. It took me a few months, but I eventually went back to work for 3 ½ days a week. The whole work / life balance seems about right and I have some flexibility if I need it.

I know that I didn't grieve 'properly' at the time, I didn't really know how to, I just got on with things – I'd pack up the car and take Sam away for weekends with family and friends, I wanted to be away and be busy.

When Sam was born, Cathy became friendly with all the other new mums in the area, they have been a godsend to be honest, one family in particular really took us under their wing. I'm the same as most men – I won't ask for help but I'll gladly accept it when it's offered. I became a regular at toddler play groups, and was "one of the mums."

I now find socialising a little difficult at times. Being with other couples inevitably makes one feel a bit awkward, but equally, going out with the lads isn't the same when they are all "escaping from the Mrs!"

Just what can you say to someone in my situation? I don't think I knew before it happened to me!

Groups like WAY (Widowed and Young) have helped me to understand that I'm not the only person going through this, it has been great for support and to meet others that have been through something similar.

Sam has just started school and is thriving. I'm very proud of him as I know his mum would be.

These are tough times but I'm no longer alone, although of course, I do feel lonely at times.

Diagnosis

At the time of diagnosis, it seems that the world might just end; it doesn't matter what side of the coin you're looking at – as someone suffering from a condition to the family of someone recently diagnosed with a life-limiting condition.

Of course, everyone reacts differently; some just get very practical while others may just want to stop there and then. However you feel, whatever it is that you want to do, your local hospice can help (unless of course it's taking a spaceship to the moon – that's quite a tall order).

The first thing to remember is that a hospice understands. As unfortunate as it is, you aren't the first person going through this, and for the foreseeable future, it's doubtful that you'll be the last.

I have spent quite some time talking to people about their experiences of a hospice, the overwhelming and perhaps most significant thing that I have learnt in that time is that for many, the hospice has been their lifeline, they have been glad of the involvement, which almost goes against the grain for the average person; when they know that a hospice is going to be involved in their care plan, they fear the worst. Only as they begin to understand, just as the hospice has involvement, do they start appreciating that contact – a number of people that I have spoken to have all mentioned that once they were in the routine of hospice care, they were very reluctant to have intervention from any other healthcare body, be that a hospital, doctor or community nurse.

Visiting a hospice for the first time can be a daunting experience, especially if you're like the many people that just think of a hospice as a place where people go to die.

I have to admit, my own naivety regarding hospices led me to feel that way when I took Nic for the first time, although looking back, perhaps it started before we visited; when we first had contact with the hospice.

For us, it was just knowing that Nic needed a hospice that made it a reality.

Andrew and Rachel

I figure that if I can't say something to my counsellor, I can't say it to anybody; she's my starting point and validates how I feel about things.

I met Rachel when I was just seventeen, I was still at school. I've only ever known living with my mum and dad or living with Rachel. Of course, that's different now.

Rachel went on to become a cancer nurse at UCH, Tottenham Court Road, her job title was Clinical Service Improvement Facilitator; it was all about improving how they cared for patients in the cancer setting; she'd often tell stories about how she had brushed someone's hair or just chatted with them – just treating people as normal human beings. That's something that seems to get missed in today's world.

She wanted to use her experience to benefit others. If I can continue that for her using *my* experience, then I'd be very proud.

I suppose my overwhelming memory of Rachel's illness was the disconnect I felt that there was between services – no one seemed to communicate, either with me or each other. But that's getting a little ahead with the story.

When Rachel was first diagnosed, it was difficult; aside from the very obvious reasons, things were complicated by the fact that the team around her were existing work colleagues and friends, in particular, her clinical nurse specialist and oncologist. It was a challenge.

We were quite fortunate in the fact that my work healthcare scheme covered us for the treatment, of course, at the time of diagnosis you just want to do everything you can – going through BUPA was surely to help with that? It wasn't so much about better treatment, more to do with the speed of the service –

going through BUPA was much faster (and although it sounds
... snobbish ... the facilities were on the whole, much cleaner).
However, there were times throughout the process that having
healthcare became an issue – the transition between the two
always seemed to be a sticking a point.

Rachel had surgery first, then chemotherapy and then
radiotherapy, there always seemed to be an issue of actually who
was meant to be looking after her. We both felt huge frustration
when trying to make appointments and meetings with the
various doctors or services and when Rachel became really ill
(the last six months), the frustration just increased.

Up until that point, I was trying to work, I was in and out of
work a lot and when Rachel had surgery, I would take all the
time off that we needed.

I distinctly remember a conversation between us where I told
her that I didn't want her to worry about anything else, she had
so much to deal with that I'd take over all of the administrative
things, I just wanted her to focus on having fun and doing nice
things. Even on the day that she died, we'd spent time decorating
for Christmas, watching strictly, eating takeaway and being silly
with the kids. She died that night.

Things were OK, we were managing but it was only really
when Rachel became paralysed from the waist down that we
thought about getting proper help. In hindsight, this is probably
where most of the problems started.

We didn't know what care we needed, where to go for it or
who to contact. We sat down with the Clinical Nurse Specialist
to discuss our options, she gave us a lot of information, although
to be honest, not all of it was correct.

She told us that care would be provided by the local health
service, GP, local nursing team and also mentioned about the
hospice and all of the additional services that we'd need.

I say that this is where the problems started and for good reason; our side of the road is controlled by Barnet council, the other side of the road is Haringey council – it's like an invisible line down the centre of the road.

Sounds easy right?

Barnet council started the process, we'd had a couple of weeks of them sorting things, only to have a phone call from them saying that it was actually Haringey's responsibility.

On top of that, we then had to deal with the issue of the third party agencies; some work for Haringey, others work for Barnet, a few cross the borough boundaries and others don't.

I got really frustrated trying to identify just *who* was meant to support us; it was by no means obvious and neither council knew either. That theme extends right through the story – even after Rachel had died, no one could tell me where I had to register the death. Why did it have to be so hard? I just wanted to register the fucking death.

Rachel lost the ability to walk while in hospital. This made things extremely difficult in so many respects. She didn't need to be in hospital, she'd reached the point where the disease was terminal, she (understandably so) just wanted to be at home. In theory, this was fine, the best thing that we could do for her, but she wasn't allowed to go home until all of the support services were in place.

There was no singular person throughout the hospital that was responsible for getting that sorted, I spent most of my time on the phone trying to organise things; we knew that we needed a hospital bed, ramp, wheelchair and the health and home support services in place, Rachel wouldn't be going anywhere until they were.

This led to a great deal of frustration for both of us. Rachel just wanted to be home with us, to have some family time, I was being passed from pillar to post. Eventually, I managed to work out who did what, which organisation to deal with and how to get them moving along, here lay the next problem; some of the equipment suppliers had a lead time to supply the equipment.

I found it odd that none of these agencies ever came out to talk to us, everything was done over the phone. We never really knew what we'd come home to; had the hospital bed arrived? Were the agencies in place? What about the wheelchair, or ramp?

The next big thing for us was that Rachel was just told that she'd be seeing the palliative care team. To her, that just simply meant death. Surely someone could have come and spoken to us about it before she went home?

When we did get to meet the palliative care team, they were absolutely fantastic, incredibly helpful.

I'm not actually sure why, but I had made the assumption that someone from the team would take over the role of the Clinical Nurse Specialist – it was the CNS who had helped us to understand what's happening.

Here again, the disjointed service started to show.

The palliative nurse was great with Rachel, she took time to speak to her about all manner of things, but is she prescribed any meds, I would then have to go to the doctors to sort them out. Surely, in this day and age, meds could just arrive?

We had the local nursing team starting to come out to us now, the first woman that came was fantastic; Rachel was really nervous about having to start building up that relationship again – the nurses in hospital knew all about what she needed, what the meds were – everything. So for this local community nurse to put Rachel's mind at ease was a big thing, for both of us.

She came twice and then rang to say that she was in the wrong borough, someone else would have to start again with her.

This was just another reinforcement of my opinion that there was just a general lack of consistent communication; one person understood and communicated with all agencies, that was me. Why can't this be better?

I eventually ended up writing a full list of who did what, their responsibilities, the meds – everything. What would happen if I wasn't around? The only person that knew all the aspects of the care was me, if someone else needed to pick it up, the only other person that they could have asked would have been Rachel, and she'd have been incensed that she'd now how to pick up her own care at the end of her own life.

Everyone that you spoke to – nurses, doctors, paramedics, professors all wanted a list of medication. Isn't it on the system? Can't they just talk to each other? View the notes?

Every time we saw the consultant, he would ask for an updated list of medication, of what treatment Rachel was getting. Why can't we just cut the nonsense and ask the only question that needs asking; "what's changed since the last time I saw you?". Everything else should be seamless, it was exactly the same, nothing different, so why do we need to go through that?

The palliative care team were great, but it did feel as though we were starting again when they first came out to us. They organised counselling for Rachel and a social worker to come out and make sure the kids were OK, from no one coming to see us, we were bombarded with people.

We'd always been very open with the kids, it hadn't been a problem for us to talk to them about Rachel's illness, they knew everything that they needed to; we didn't hide away from telling them.

The first social worker did the usual – "Tell me about the situation, what I need to know", whereas the second one had actually read the notes and gave us some good advice. I guess the only down side was that then she would tell us what we *should* be doing, which kind of made us feel that we were wrong if we hadn't done it, or if we did it differently.

The final piece in the jigsaw was someone coming in the morning and evening to help me with Rachel. I'd have to say that they were great, really helpful and friendly, the only thing being that more often than not, you wouldn't see the same person twice and I feel that is important; for a stranger to come in and take care of someone's intimate needs, there should be some sort of relationship there, with a different person each time, you're never going to get that.

It was an incredibly frustrating time, I remember Rachel telling me one day that I'd be so much better off without her, just because she could see how much effort went in to caring for her.

Whilst it hurt and upset me, I suppose I can see why she said it; it was a huge effort to care for her, the relationship with the kids was a little distant – Rachel was (and had to be) my number one priority. I do feel that some of that could have been alleviated if there was a one professional that could take over the responsibility for organising everything. I was exhausted, both emotionally and physically, just existing. I wanted to do everything I could for Rachel, I refused the offer of counselling because I knew that would just break me; I needed to be strong right now, I could pick up the pieces afterward.

Weirdly, Rachel and I did have a conversation about the fact that we both thought the experience couldn't have been any better (aside from the obvious of course). I know that sounds odd, but … my healthcare scheme was good, Harley Street was only six miles away, Rachel knew the nursing team, we were OK financially, work were understanding – it could have been much worse.

I genuinely think that we couldn't have done anything more.

I have to say, I wasn't keen on asking for help, even when our parents were there, I'd rather have done things myself. I just wanted to do everything that *I* could, I naturally wanted the best for Rachel, I'm sure that I created a lot of extra stress for myself, but that was the way it had to be.

One of the most difficult things was just keeping on top of the meds; I'd spend hours sorting them, it was a constant worry and I couldn't let anyone else do it. Besides, the only other person that knew the extent of the meds and the schedule was Rachel.

Rachel's death had a profound impact on me.

I reflect a lot on life in general, I'm learning to be a single adult but I have two kids; it's strange to be learning who I am as a person, but with two kids, two dogs and a house.

The relationship that I have with my kids has changed, I have got to know them better and our relationship is wonderful.

I was recently asked at work what my greatest achievement was, without hesitation or thought, I answered it was how I'd looked after Rachel.

Through her work, Rachel had spoken at great length about dignity in death, I believe that we did that for her.

Palliative Care

P alliative care is defined by NICE (National Institute for Clinical Excellence) as the following:

The active holistic care of patients with advanced progressive illness. Management of pain and other symptoms and provision of psychological, social and spiritual support is paramount. The goal of palliative care is achievement of the best quality of life for patients and their families. Many aspects of palliative care are also applicable earlier in the course of the illness in conjunction with other treatments.

Quite a mouthful I'm sure you'll agree, and really not that clear, or at least not to me.

However, the simplified version makes things much clearer; if you're suffering from an illness that can't be cured, palliative care is used to make you as comfortable as you can be, it does this by managing your pain and other symptoms.

It also includes social, spiritual and psychological care for you, your family and your carers. It is a 'holistic' approach to care and management of an illness.

What does this mean in real terms?

That's a difficult question, or certainly not an easy answer, but as a layman, I can't help but be drawn to the phrase 'open minded' care.

How often do you hear about people with an illness wanting to spend time with their beloved pet for example? And when they *do* get that chance, their whole face lights up, their demeanour changes and even just for a few minutes, they seem … healthy?

That is a perfect example of palliative care in action.

The old phrase about laughter being the best medicine would now be considered as palliative care. Of course, traditional medicine is used to combat the effects of an illness, the actual acute medical need, but treating an illness is so much more than medical.

We should also consider that while treating an illness with a holistic approach can only ever be a good thing, the palliative care could also help you come to terms with the illness or the effects of that illness; it's almost the over-arching umbrella under which treatment (in any form) comes.

Palliative care aims to:

- Provide relief from pain and other distressing symptoms
- Offer a support system to help patients live as actively as possible until death
- Integrate the psychological and spiritual aspects of patient care
- Provide a support system to help the family cope during the patient's illness and in their bereavement
- Affirm life and regard dying as a normal process
- Maintain the patient's dignity at all times

Danny and Emma

I met Emma through my job as a bike courier; I used to deliver small parcels to the company she worked at, she was the receptionist there.

We kind of hit it off pretty quickly, I always felt there was something there between us, but in all honesty, I didn't have the brass to ask her out on a date.

She was good looking, funny, (and of course, I'd have to say sexy!) and seemed pretty grounded – what would she see in me? A bloke that makes his living from riding a pushbike all day.

As time went on, we progressed from "Sign here" to "Hello you, got another one" and then "Wow, what a great day" (being British, of course the weather played a natural part in our conversations!).

It took me a few months to work out whether she was single, even longer to ask her out on a date (which she immediately agreed to) and that was kind of it really.

She always used to take the mickey out of me for not asking her out sooner, she used to say that she thought I wasn't interested in women because I didn't see the signs; I just thought she was friendly.

Our first date was in a little place just off New Street, we had a bite to eat (I remember thinking that for such a small girl, she couldn't half pack some food in) and a couple of drinks, I thought it was quite romantic but Em never really seemed that … enthusiastic … if I'm honest. Whatever I did, it must have been right because after a goodnight kiss, we said our goodbyes and within an hour, I'd had a text saying that she'd had a wonderful night and wanted to do it again. Get in!

We didn't get to see each other for a week or so after that, not even through work, but we had a fair bit of contact through texting, it was nice – feeling a little smile creep over me when I saw her name pop up on my screen, the only thing was that I found myself waiting for her next reply and when it did come through, I rather stupidly tried to check my phone while riding and almost ran into the back of a bus. The things we do when we're in love.

We started seeing each other more regularly, but it was difficult at times because Em had a young son, she couldn't just pop out and I couldn't just go round; she was understandably very wary of letting me in to her son's life. We both kind of knew (or at least hoped) that we had a future, but then you don't get involved with someone expecting it to go wrong do you? But even with us both feeling that way, we decided to take things easy, mainly for the sake of Liam.

I think there were times that both of us just wanted to get on with it – tell Liam and then we could start having some sort of normal time together, but for one reason or another, I don't really know why now, we held back until we were both sure it was absolutely right. Em had been dropping my name in conversation in the hope that when she did finally say "this is Danny", it wouldn't be too much of a surprise. We think that worked; Liam didn't seem phased by it all, we both wondered if we should have (could have?) done it sooner.

Very soon, we were almost inseparable; if we weren't at work, we were together, usually at Emma's place, even though it was ridiculously small, but that didn't matter. I still had my own place, it was bigger than Em's but she was adamant that we wouldn't be there that much due to the 'memories' of my ex. I can sort of get that, but let's be honest, that's definitely more of a woman thing than a bloke thing. Shit. Can I say that? I don't want to offend people, but ... I just think that on the whole, blokes aren't that bothered by that sort of stuff.

Anyway, we got to the point where I was spending all of my time there, we spoke about moving in together but in all honesty, her place was just too small for the three of us (and associated stuff), we had to look at finding our own place, it would be a fresh start for all of us.

This was a big thing for me, my own place was exactly that – mine. Even when my ex lived with me, it was always my place, never hers or ours, just mine. I guess I was quite selfish like that.

I think that's where I'm lucky; yes, I've been through some shit after Em died, but it was her that taught me to love properly, that showed me just what love was about – none of this nonsense about this thing being mine, that thing being hers, it was all just ours.

We started looking at houses, somewhere with a bit more space, we both wanted somewhere a little more rural, but it couldn't be too far out of the city – I *could* drive, but didn't; I didn't own a car only my pushbike and a motorbike. I knew that at some point I'd have to grow up though and succumb to four-wheels, I just didn't want to feel that I was being made to do it.

I look back now at that sort of thing – about feeling like I was being made to do things and I long for such feelings. It all seems so ... petty. I wish I still had that choice.

Along with moving in together, we started talking about other things being more permanent. Marriage had never crossed my mind at all, I wasn't against the idea, it's just that it never felt right before. But wouldn't it be great to move in to our new home together as man and wife?

As it happens, that didn't work out, purely because of the stress of not just moving house, but moving in 'together', me becoming a proper dad (we sorted all the paperwork for me to be Liam's dad) and a hundred and one other things. I'd have to say that life was good. I can honestly say that I'd never been happier and I know that was the case for Emma also. We were just meant to be, simple as that.

So what changed?

On the morning of June 17th 2010, Emma was involved in a car accident, although technically, I've since learned that 'accident' isn't the correct word; no longer is it an RTA (Road Traffic Accident), it's an RTC (Road Traffic Collision) because someone is always to blame, it's never an accident. Bizarre.

In this case, someone was definitely to blame.

I've often asked myself whether I'd have felt better about it if it had been a random accident, or if she'd been ill, or even if it had been her choice – all of those scenarios have a better reason than some pissed up bloke losing control of his car.

For a long time, I sat and thought about the probability of it all; being involved in a fatal car accident – low, being hit by a drunken driver – low, being hit by a drunk driver at 8.30 in the morning and suffering fatal injuries – non-existent. Except of course, it wasn't non-existent.

You may have guessed that I'm still angry about it. That man didn't just take one life that day, he destroyed three.

...

44

Here we are, six years later.

Legally, I became a dad all those years ago when I signed the paperwork, technically, I'd say that I only really became a dad the day that Em died.

Both of our families have been great, they've supported me every step of the way, no matter how ... badly behaved I was.

I'd say that being a dad has changed my perspective, but I'd guess that also goes for the experience that I've been through.

I wouldn't change my relationship with Liam, but equally there are times when I wonder whether my life would be different if I didn't have him to think about. I feel guilty for even thinking that, never mind saying it out loud, I'm hoping that it's part of the grief process, people say that it is.

I realise that there are millions of people around the world in a similar situation, my heart goes out to all of them.

When Jamie approached me about adding my story to the book, I was unsure; living with it is one thing, but sharing it is something completely new to me. The reason why I agreed is to say that whilst I still have these bad times, I can tell you that things really do get better. Really.

Carer Support

For the purpose of the book, when we refer to the 'carer', we are talking about the informal or family carers that are so vital in the healthcare process, not just in terms of looking after a love one, but in actually supporting the NHS and healthcare system.

It is said that carers provide up to £132bn of support to the UK and that 89% of carers have suffered a negative impact on their own health as a direct result of caring for someone.

Another statistic could be that there are approximately 6.5 million carers in the UK. Are you one of them?

Strangely, many carers don't actually recognise themselves as such; they're just looking after a loved one.

But why is it important to recognise that you've taken over the role of a carer?

For many people, caring for someone isn't a choice, it's a fact. This means that sleeves get rolled up, the job gets done and no more is said about it.

In theory, this is OK, millions of people around the world do it every day, and it's a fact of life, but learning to recognise that you're the main carer is a vital step to understanding (and recognising) that you need to look after yourself just as much as your loved one. Admittedly, you may not have an acute medical need, but research shows us that what can start as stress or physical hard work, can soon turn into a medical crisis if it isn't monitored. Who looks after your loved one if you can't?

Hospices (amongst other organisations) recognise that this happens all too often, and that unless action is taken, a bad situation can become worse.

Caring for someone 24-hours a day has been described as a "superhuman" effort. Not only is it physically demanding, but the mental strain it can put you under can break a person. I say that from experience – it wasn't just coming to terms with Nic's illness, it was the lack of sleep, the feeling that the onus was on me, of understanding medication routines & times; dealing with all of that on top of your regular daily routine means very little respite.

How can the hospice help?

There are many things that a hospice can do to help. If nothing else, they can offer respite care, meaning that you get a chance to have some time for yourself – that could be filled by resting, catching up on your sleep or even filling out paperwork – the point being that the responsibility has been lifted or alleviated and even as a temporary measure, that lifting of the onus can be felt, almost physically.

When we are caring for a loved one, we tend to put our own needs aside; we go into a kind of auto-pilot, thinking that nobody else can look after our loved one as well as we can. This in turn becomes a vicious circle and we can start to go into meltdown.

Further than that though, the hospice is a good source of information and it doesn't necessarily have to be medical.

On the face of it, there are many and numerous organisations offering knowledge or support, but as we've already touched on, many of these organisations aren't that easy to get through to, at least not to a genuine (and caring) human that can understand exactly what it is that you're going through.

Whilst there is a wealth of information on the internet, we have to consider two things; not everyone uses the internet and there is an old saying that goes something like "you don't know what you don't know".

In other words, information could be at your fingertips, but there is a good chance that there are many things you haven't even thought about because they haven't *needed* thinking about. This is where a hospice can really help you out – just by discussing the process, the help and the considerations – there's a good chance that you'll learn more information from an informal chat with a professional than you will anywhere else.

Signposting

Don't be confused by the term. 'Signposting' is just about directions (just as a road signpost). This fits with the not knowing what you need to know area, the two are closely linked. Understanding or knowing where to find information can be key to reducing the anxiety felt, either as a carer or as someone going through a life-limiting illness.

Putting it plainly, your world has just fallen apart and you need information on how to build it back up again, but even the most knowledgeable of people can't know *everything*!

A hospice is a trusted resource for information, either directly or indirectly, and it's the indirect part where signposting is used.

Pointing you in the right direction to find credible information is a skill in its own right; you don't need to know how James Knox III from Utah cured his illness by rubbing his middle toe with a banana for example, but there also needs to be an element of understanding exactly what it is you want to know – you may very well have an interest in therapies that aren't usually considered for your condition for example, or joining a support group for a particular condition that not many have heard of, or you may want just plain old facts about an illness.

Of course, we should also consider that as your world has just been turned upside down, you may not feel up to spending hours researching something, you probably won't have the time and let's be honest, you may not want to wade through pages and pages of 'information' just to find that one key piece that fits your need.

Jim and Christine

I was 21 when I met my wife, we were together 48 years in total, married for 45 of them. We got married 21ˢᵗ September 1968.

The whole cancer journey started in 2004 when the wife was diagnosed with breast cancer. She had to have a mastectomy and then both chemo and radiotherapy. When she had her prosthetic breast fitted, we used to joke about it, called it "The Buddy". It was the same when she lost her hair and had a hair piece – that was the "rugrat" and got thrown around like a rubber ball – "here, you have it".

Everything was OK for about ten years, but then she started feeling sick and had pain in her back. She went to get checked out and the cancer had come back in her bones. The consultant said that she'll keep her going for as long as she can.

You hear those words and you just *know*.

Another round of full-strength chemotherapy, which was really knocking her about. I was trying to work and look after her, I had to plead for time off work, taking most of it as holiday. It was around this time that my dad died, and then mum was diagnosed with dementia. Everyone tells me that they don't know how I coped, but you just do, don't you? There isn't a choice, you just find the strength and get on with it.

The wife was originally from Wales, so didn't have any other family around to help look after her, everything was down to me. I was juggling work, mum, the wife; but I did it.

In amongst all of that, we had to move home. 38 years in the same house, but the illness made it difficult – she couldn't get up the stairs so we moved in to a bungalow. We were only there for 7 months before the end.

She battled the cancer for about twelve months, eventually dying in the George Eliot hospital on the 4th January 2014.

People say that before someone dies they get better, at least for a short time. On the Thursday before, the wife sat up and spoke to one of the nurses, telling her that she was well enough to go home, providing she could stop on the way home to pay the gas bill.

I have to say, all of the nurses, doctors and MacMillan nurses were great, I couldn't fault them at all. It was one of the Macmillan nurses that suggested I contact my local hospice – The Mary Ann Evans Hospice.

I really wasn't sure whether to go along or not, it was only really after my daughter told me that it takes a stronger person to go there and talk about it than it does to sit at home and stare at four walls that I decided to go.

My first meeting was with Gill, she's the Chaplain at the hospice. It was good, certainly good enough for me to go back at least. I soon found myself in a group; two women, me and another man, along with a volunteer. Three out of the four of us had all been married within a couple of hours of each other – same day, same month and same year. Imagine that? Complete strangers with such a thing in common.

I now attend a regular group, we talk about anything and everything; I've certainly told people things there that I wouldn't tell anyone else. It's a good release.

I know that I'm in a slightly different group than the other contributors for this book; my kids were grown up when their mum died, but that doesn't really make it easier, perhaps a little easier for me, but not for them.

Obviously both of them loved their mum dearly, but my daughter was really close to her, she tends to talk quite openly about the experience, whereas my son plays things much closer to his chest. I've always said that whatever feels right for them *is* what's best for them. They both know that I'm here if they want to talk about it.

I've found that the best way of dealing with it is to just keep occupied; keep your mind busy so you don't have time to dwell on the experience, you'll never forget it, but you don't need to relive it every day.

Recreational Therapy

R ecreational therapy encompasses many different subjects, and whereas most of the topics included in this book are aimed at both patient and carer, recreational therapy is solely designed and used from the patient's perspective.

From a non-professional view point, I considered recreational therapy as something designed to give a patient some time out of the medical cycle, to perhaps give a carer some respite and to give the patient some social time that isn't all about illness, drugs, routine and health.

Having spoken to some therapists and carried out a little research, I can see that I wasn't completely wrong, but there is so much more to it than I knew.

The primary purpose of recreational therapy is to use a range of activities such as arts & crafts, music, dance and drama to restore, remediate and rehabilitate to improve functioning and independence. This in turn helps to reduce or eliminate the effects of an illness or disability, thereby improving upon the general health and wellbeing of a patient.

A therapist will work with the patient to try and help restore motor, social and cognitive abilities, build confidence and develop coping skills.

John and Lucy

I first met Lucy on a night out with some friends from work; we'd been to the local pub for a few beers and she was there with her friends (completely separately). We got chatting by accident (well, she trod on my foot, we got chatting – we later used to joke about her doing it deliberately).

We were together for nearly eighteen years in total, married for fourteen of them and we had two boys who were ten and thirteen when she passed.

I think having the boys there helped me when it happened. People have said to me that it must have been hell to go through and still have to be there for the boys, but without them, I'm sure I would have lost the plot completely. They kept me anchored, I had no choice but to get on with things and look after them – if I didn't do it, who would?

For so long after Lucy died, I was angry. I couldn't get over the question of why her? What had she done wrong? Even going past that, why US? After all, it wasn't just her – this knocked us *all* for six.

I don't know whether that is selfish, grief or justified; people always say that whatever you're feeling, it is right for you. I would say that now, I'm not quite as angry about it, but still just numb.

Actually, that probably isn't right. Yes, I do have those days where things are numb, where I just get through the day like some sort of robot, but I have noticed that slowly, I am getting more of the odd days where good things happen and I recognise that they are good things – I think it's the recognition of them that makes them so significant.

Much of the detail is quite hazy, I think it's because it's something that I've tried not to think about over the years – you know, kind of like *trying* to forget about it. Of course, you'll never truly forget, that's always going to be a part of my life that I have to live with, but that's exactly what I do – live with it.

I started noticing a difference in Lucy, only small things, but at the time I put it down to the stresses of everyday life and work; she would become quite snappy, not quite angry but maybe on the verge of it. For some time, I wondered whether our marriage was in trouble, it was that kind of atmosphere where it seemed that whatever anyone said or did (particularly me), it would be wrong. A short temper, or perhaps lack of tolerance. It's quite difficult trying to quantify it, but that is the best way I could describe it – a relationship going bad but neither party wanting to actually say it so you just end up sniping at each other.

Looking back now, I would say that what alerted us to something being actually wrong was that she became rather clumsy to start with, like tripping over her feet. The first couple of times it happened was just a joke – "enjoy your trip" and all of that, but it became more common (we aren't talking falling over every day, but what was maybe once a fortnight became once a week).

We had spoken about the clumsiness, she brushed it off as tiredness mainly, and that fitted with (what I know now to be the next 'symptom') being tired all the time; it didn't seem to matter how much sleep Lucy got, she was always tired. She had gone from being a bubbly, hard working (and to a degree, hard living) woman to someone that just wanted to sit and do nothing, except for watching TV or a bit of reading.

It was around this point that we started to recognise that something could be wrong. Neither of us actually knew that there was anything medically wrong, but we both knew that she wasn't right, certainly not her usual self. It took us a few months to act upon it though – we both thought that she was physically healthy, just that she wasn't her usual self, nothing to rush to the doctors for – it would just be as and when she had another appointment she'd mention it.

Looking back at it now, maybe if we'd acted earlier, the outcome might have been different? I try not to think too much about stuff like that, because it really isn't helpful, but it is something that I have thought about.

The doctor didn't seem overly bothered by anything, but did say that she'd monitor the situation and to let her know if things got any worse. We carried on like this for some time, nothing seemed to get worse but it certainly never got any better. Lucy was full of lethargy, just never really wanting to do anything and we accepted that it was just the daily grind. Things really changed when she collapsed as she got up from her chair one day.

We made an appointment with the doctor for the following day and insisted that they do something – we couldn't just accept that this was just normal life now; collapsing after no exertion wasn't normal for anyone, regardless.

I forget how long it took to get an appointment with a consultant at the local hospital, some months for sure. Finally, there was something actually happening and Lucy went for a CT scan of her head, the idea was to make sure there was nothing untoward happening with her brain. As far as we were concerned, this was just routine, in fact, she was told just that – nothing to be alarmed at.

That is of course until the results came through.

The results showed that there was an issue, they didn't know what; they would need to investigate further, which would be done asap. Within two weeks we had another appointment with another consultant, he did his best to reassure us that everything would be OK, and for a time, we did feel reassured – it really seemed as though it was no big deal.

I understand that doctors aren't just going to say that your world is about to go pear shaped, but ... we had no idea of the severity of what was about to hit us.

At the time, neither of us knew about any of the medical terms used; we were told a Grade 4 tumour and to us, at least for a short moment, that meant it wasn't too bad – 4 out of 10 meant less than half (if that makes sense?). Of course, for those of you that *don't* know, the scale doesn't go that high – 4 is the maximum.

When we learned what that actually meant, "GRADE 4", we were devastated. It seemed that any hopes we had were just flushed away; one moment things are OK, the very next instant and life has changed, never to be the same again, nothing will ever be *OK* again. A second in time was all it took for our lives to change.

Of course, we looked at all the options, including trying to raise funds to go to America for treatment. There was no actual logical reason why America would be different; it's just an assumption that everything pioneering in the world of cancer seems to originate from there, but having looked into it, that turns out to be not necessarily the case. Besides, we aren't talking about a few thousand dollars, not even tens of thousands; a single CT scan could cost anywhere up to $3,000.

To watch the illness take over Lucy's body was something that will live with me forever. The gradual decline of the person that I knew, that I loved, that I was meant to grow old with was something horrific.

I guess that 'gradual' is all in the perspective; the rest of the time that we had together was never going to be enough, but also, it seemed that something changed on a daily basis; from losing her motor skills and being unable to walk to losing the ability to control her toilet needs.

Our life was now one long blur of hospitals, medication, treatment, lack of sleep, care … the illness took over *our* lives, not just Lucy's. I honestly can't remember different days where things happened, it was just one long event. I'd had to give up work sometime previously, this put even more pressure on us – we had no money coming in, we were claiming benefits but they weren't much, in fact that's one of the biggest things that I have taken from this whole thing; people caring for someone need much more support from the government financially – your bills don't stop just because your life is turning to poo. At this point though, I would have physically fought anyone if they'd have tried to demand money.

All in all, we had about twenty months. Care wise, it felt like a lifetime, but of course, if someone had said to me "we can give you another year together", I'd have taken that in a heartbeat.

Looking back at the whole thing now, I'm still quite dazed, but life does indeed go on.

That was extremely hard for me to accept – "Life goes on". It does. Despite all the loving messages and support from family and friends, you find that they move on quicker than you can, which of course is natural, but sometimes you wish it wasn't. I find significant dates to be an awful thing; wanting people to say "I'm thinking of you" and yet wanting to forget it, not wanting people to make a fuss and bring it all back up again. I guess that will change over time.

The boys are doing well, despite not having a mother figure around, although I do have a 'girlfriend' (that is such a weird statement, one that at this age, I never thought I'd say – it feels like being back at school!). Their school has been fantastic, I can't fault them at all, supporting not only the boys, but me as well. I've made quite a few good friends since Lucy died, it's good that they don't really know what happened (well, certainly none of the details) – it's like my life is starting again to a certain degree.

Complementary Therapy

For some people, therapies such as Reflexology or Reiki are mystical hocus-pocus, whilst others would stake their world on them. However you choose to view them, I would recommend that you at least try what's on offer.

I must confess to being in the former group of people before I started on this journey (although I had some experience of acupuncture before Nic was ill); someone placing their hands near you and expecting to gain benefit was ... not something that a fact based engineer was prepared to accept as viable or realistic.

However ... whilst I may not shout from the rooftops about just how wonderful the experience can be, I would say that after trying it, I do feel it has benefits.

This isn't to denigrate therapies such as this in anyway, but just looking at it all from the perspective of cold hard facts; if I do X then Y will happen, guaranteed.

I can say that whenever I had Reiki, my body relaxed to the point of sleep (sometimes in the middle of the session!) and that the day I had Reiki, I would actually get a full night's sleep, which even now, 8 years later, eludes me.

Also, whenever the therapist's hands went near my ears, they would twitch uncontrollably. Let's make it clear, there was absolutely no contact with them; not even gently brushing the little hairs (as a man of more mature years gets) sprouting out from them.

For me, I can whole heartedly say that complementary therapy had a huge and positive impact on my life at that time, that is why I would always tell people to try it, no matter how sceptical they may be!

Reiki

R eiki is a translation of the Japanese relating to 'universal life energy'; it is believed that all living things have an energy flowing through us, and Reiki will help that energy flow through us in an uninterrupted manner, balancing our energy and restoring our wellbeing.

The treatment is completely non-intrusive; laying (or sitting) on a suitable platform, the Reiki master places their hands on or near the fully-clothed recipient at key points. The person receiving the treatment may experience a number of different sensations, from the feeling of localised heat, relaxation, drowsiness, a tingling on their skin and perhaps may even see colours.

One of the most widely reported affects after the session is deep relaxation, which is certainly the case for me.

Reflexology

A gain, completely non-intrusive and other than your socks, no need to bare any skin. Some practitioners have embraced technology and use reflexology 'boots' whilst others prefer to work by hand.

From my own perspective, the boots certainly were a strange experience, but I much preferred the traditional method of 'hands-on' massage.

Reflexology is based on the theory that different points on the feet (the theory extends to feet, lower legs, hands, face and even the ears, but most people practice reflexology on the feet) link to different points throughout the body.

Again, in my own experience, I can state that there was always one particular point on my right foot that when pressed, would *always* trigger the same response in my hand.

The idea is to treat a person as part of a holistic therapy and routine; there is no one single definitive answer or cure that reflexology will provide; practitioners are skilled therapists that work *with you* to establish what the benefits could be.

The theory behind the practice is that reflexology will help to restore your balance; people say they feel more relaxed or notice a reduction in tension, perhaps even sleeping better or just have an overall sense of better wellbeing.

Acupuncture

A cupuncture dates back for thousands of years, but for many, the thought of looking (feeling?) like a human pin cushion puts them off even considering it.

Of course, different people have a varied sense of feeling and different parts of the body will naturally be more sensitive, but research carried out shows that most people feel absolutely no discomfort whilst being treated.

Acupuncture has been used to treat a wide range of conditions, be that spiritual, mental or physical.

Unlike many complementary therapies, acupuncture is available on the NHS, but we should clarify that acupuncture is classified in two different ways; traditional acupuncture and Western medical acupuncture.

Traditional acupuncture uses the theory that the body has its own energy called Qi (pronounced as 'Chee'), and it is the disruption of that Qi that causes problems, whereas Western medicinal acupuncture relies on stimulating the sensory nerves located within our body, this in turn creates our body's natural pain killers; endorphins.

Hypnotherapy

H ypnotherapy is used worldwide to induce a state of mind that makes you more suggestive and open; this can end up with 'hilarious' videos of someone believing that they are a chicken *or* it can be put to use in a much better way.

Studies have shown that hypnotherapy can help reduce some of the associated effects of cancer treatments, these could stiff limbs, sore joints or even vomiting.

As with all complementary therapies, you may find it helps enormously or feel little benefit at all; you often hear that some people just aren't suited to it.

From talking with a number of therapists, it would seem that those more open to suggestion in the first place will generally see more benefit.

The therapy itself is often misunderstood; people believing that once you're placed under a state of hypnosis, there is no coming out of it until the practitioner allows you to.

This simply isn't the case; you are always aware, in control and able to stop at any time simply by opening your eyes – this isn't a staged pantomime act.

Putting aside the potential benefits of reduced pain or nausea, most people that have had professional hypnotherapy all comment on how relaxed and calm they feel after the treatment.

As with the other treatments, it's completely non-invasive and no need to shed any clothes; just wear something comfortable.

Other forms of complementary therapy

There are numerous other forms of complementary therapy, ranging from aromatherapy through to yoga, and of course, not all hospices are in the position to offer these, but talking to them will at least give you a clearer picture of what they can do for you.

It's worth remembering that most forms of therapy are there to help you relax, give you some respite and improve your day to day life.

There are many advocates for complementary therapy as an alternative to traditional medicine, and whilst we respect those opinions, there doesn't seem to be any hard and fast rules as to how they work, the benefit they give (medicinally) or the effectiveness of them. A combination of treatments and therapies is usually the way forward for most people, if you have any questions, doubts or concerns, talk to your team at your local hospice.

Mark and Sophia

I was on my gap year, the plan was to sample the delights of the world (and we aren't talking about culture here) whilst I was young, free and single – the whole cliché. As I have grown up, I have found a distaste for some of the phrases that I'll use to describe me, my life and what I wanted then, but it's probably the best way to tell my story, after all, that's who I was.

I was a bit of a 'Jack the Lad' when I was younger (that's the first phrase out of the way), always wanting to party and find a woman that I could 'connect' with (and there's the second). The intention was to leave uni and travel the world just doing exactly that. For the first month or two, everything was going to plan; a girl in every port (bugger, that's a third) and a hangover to prove what a good night we'd had; what could be better than that?

The problem started when we went stateside, to the west coast (surely every good road trip should take in The Golden State? California in case you're wondering). It had long been on my list of places to visit, not only did it seem to be one of *the* coolest places on the planet, but it was home to some of the big tech companies that I would love to get involved with. California *had* to happen.

We were out at a bar, or to be more precise, a pub; this was an English themed bar (Jacks or something similar – I guess from 'Union Jack'), the atmosphere was pretty good and surprisingly, there were a number of British people there, even more surprising was that nearly everyone spoke with a plum in their mouth – surely this was for effect; gosh, how very quaint, tea (with the emphasis on the T E), Windsor Palace … it seemed as though most were distant relations to the Queen or Prince Philip, or at least that's what they wanted everyone to think, including Sophia, one of the servers. (I must admit, I was ever so slightly guilty of cranking up the posho when Sophia came round).

I'd love to tell you that we fell in love instantly and I stayed in America and did the whole 'American Dream' thing, but the simple reality is that although we (Sophia and I) got on well, and undoubtedly had a spark, she was never in a million years going to date me because I was going to be out of there within a few weeks.

I accepted that, despite having feelings for her that were silly – we hadn't even been on a date, yet here I was, constantly thinking of her and wanting to spend time with only her.

We kept in touch for a while, probably a few months, but then it just kind of stopped, entirely my fault I would say, although of course at the time, I thought she just didn't care enough to chase me.

Yes, I really was that arrogant.

Fast forward a couple of years and I'm back in England, living in Oxford. I was out just doing the daily grind stuff; domestic chores and shopping, all very boring, but as I wandered past a local coffee shop, there was a loud banging on the window.

When I looked to see what was happening, I couldn't make head nor tail of the situation – every single face in the coffee shop had turned toward the window, staring at the passers-by, trying to understand what was going on also. It felt like minutes had passed (but in reality it must have been seconds) before I spotted Sophia.

It took a while for my brain to engage – staring at Sophia, mouth open, trying to put the pieces together – a face I knew (and quite possibly loved at one point), sitting in a small coffee shop in Oxford, my brain working overtime thanks to only associating this face with America.

This just couldn't be happening.

She was over here on holiday with her Mum, just taking in the sights of Oxford.

I guess that some people would call this fate, that this was meant to be, but I honestly can't say that, because then I'd have to also believe that her death was also "just meant to be".

Either way, she was on day 4 of a two week holiday (vacation), as far as I was concerned, that gave me just over a week with her (respecting the fact that she couldn't just abandon her mum).

It was pretty evident that the spark was still there for both of us. But of course, she was reluctant because it was now her that would be disappearing again. Aaaargh.

We spent time together, and in what I can only describe as a self-respect bypass, I pretty much pleaded with her.

Happily, we did start seeing each other (no naughty business though!) but in what seemed like a minute, it was time for her to go home. Whilst this was pretty devastating, I was fairly certain that I had found my 'one'; I would move heaven and earth to make this work.

I can't pretend that it was easy, but we did get through it and we did make it work. Sophia eventually coming to live in England (with me) was just … perfect.

(Of course, there was a minor moment of "Oh sh★★, just what did I tell her back in the U.S.? – Was there anything going to come back and haunt me? Third cousin, twice removed from the Queen?)

I have to say that life was pretty good, we had a nice house, good jobs; I suppose you'd call it *comfortable*. I think we were lucky to be honest, in so many respects.

We started talking about children, initially I was reluctant, not for any other reason than I'd never thought about it, I didn't really see myself as a father, that was for older people – you had to be a grown up.

As the realisation dawned on me that I was indeed, a grown up, in a full-time career, with responsibilities such as a mortgage, I started to understand that perhaps children could be a good thing for us, so we bought a dog!

It wasn't much later that we found out that Sophia was pregnant, we were thrilled, anxious, scared even, but it was what we both wanted, more than anything. Happiness ruled the roost.

It wasn't until Lydia was about three did things begin to change.

Sophia had worked hard to get back her pre-pregnancy body, not so much through exercise but being careful what she ate, it seemed that every day was a punishment to be honest – we weren't allowed 'snacky' type food in the house, nothing too loaded with calories (read taste) and only the very occasional take away; for me, the week is best rounded off with an Indian takeaway and a beer (I do like a glass of wine, but not with Indian!).

All that went out of the window, but I was happy (well, willing) to do that because I knew how much it meant to Sophia.

Not wishing to get too graphic, Sophia's toilet habits weren't great, but she had just assumed that it was her body protesting about the lack of yummy things, it's only really when her weight just carried on going down did she (we) think there may be some sort of problem.

Contrary to what many people say, I have to say that the doctor (GP) was excellent, nothing was too much trouble, but more than that, we had the impression that we weren't just being brushed off with the old favourite – "it's a virus".

It took a while to get to the bottom of it, mainly because Sophia didn't fit the regular picture of who does or doesn't get bowel cancer; all of the regular indicators didn't fit with her at all (OK, she liked a drink in moderation, she smoked up until she was pregnant with Lydia but that really was it), there was absolutely no reason behind it, I think that's what makes it so hard to accept.

So, bowel cancer was the diagnosis, life settled down a little; we knew what we were doing and how best to get on with things. Sophia was extremely well organised; everything colour coded, in a spreadsheet and planned out, she'd even set time aside for unforeseen things, it was as though she was just running a big project, quite remarkable.

Looking back at it, perhaps this was just her way of dealing with it, just keeping busy, her mind occupied and not thinking about anything else. To be honest, it seemed to work; it looked as though the treatment was working, she was getting healthier, or at least she was for a time, she had definitely picked up a little, you can imagine the relief.

Having spoken to others in a similar situation, this seems to be the pattern – unfortunately, so does the next part ...

Things took a turn for the worse, the treatment knocked her about something silly, the cancer was spreading and it didn't want to stop, there really wasn't much we could do other than make her daily life a little less challenging. I know she felt guilty at this, everyone that supported us tried to make her understand that she needed to concentrate on her, none of us begrudged what we were doing, we loved her and wanted to look after her as best as possible.

Of course, one of the biggest problems that we had was her family were some 6,000 odd miles away, they couldn't really just pop over for a day or two, they had to time their visits to coincide with potential markers / events. To try and cut down on costs, they would be put up at friends or relatives of ours, everyone was great, they just pulled together, exactly as you'd hope your closest friends and relatives would do in a crisis situation.

Aside from the very obvious, I think we were quite lucky really; everyone (including the NHS) just made things happen, there was never a moment where caring for Sophia was an issue, or where the treatment process failed, everything worked just as it should.

People knock the NHS, but I for one have nothing but admiration for them, I won't hear a bad word said against them.

Sophia's funeral was perhaps the most difficult aspect of it all, purely from a logistical point of view – trying to get her family over from America and Canada was hellish. It's an odd thing to say, but we were helped by the fact that there were delays in the process – it seemed that a lot of people were waiting to be buried.

After Sophia's death, I took some time away from everything and everyone, just me and Lydia. I felt that I needed to be there for her, if I'm honest, she was probably a little neglected (attention wise) whilst we were going through it all. I spent about seven months just being there for her constantly, I'd be there in the morning to take her to school, there to collect her from school, we'd cook dinner together, go through her school work and generally just be silly.

I thought that was something that she needed, but I guess it's also something that I needed.

About 18 months later, I decided that there wasn't that much in England for me anymore, yes I had some good friends and loving family, but I wanted to be somewhere different, I also thought it important that Lydia got to know her American grandparents. We sold up, lock stock and barrel and moved to the U.S.

I feel OK with the situation, of course I would rather have Sophia by my side, for Lydia to have a mother, to share all of those wonderful moments of our child growing up, but it's not going to happen is it?

For my part, I'm glad that we had the time that we did; the chance of us bumping into each other again was infinitesimally small, but we did. That's why it was so special, because everything just happened, and no, I still don't believe in fate!

Bereavement Service

Losing someone close to you can bring about indescribable feelings and pain, both mentally and physically. Dealing with that pain and *those* feelings makes it hard to live any sort of life afterward, at least for the foreseeable future.

I was told that "no matter what you're feeling, it's right for *you*". There are no right or wrong feelings, I've spoken to people that feel guilty because they haven't shed a single tear, others (like me) had a complete breakdown and couldn't cope with anything afterward. None of that is wrong.

However you deal with the situation, or perhaps process the grief, that has to be the right way for you – don't try and force anything, let nature take its own course.

Of course, that sounds easy to say, a different version of "what will be, will be", but that doesn't really help does it?

Bereavement support won't give you any magic answers, it just *can't* make things all OK again, there is no cure.

But, what it can do is help you to get a better understanding of what it is you've been through, of how your body might react, of certain things to be aware of; it's a source of knowledge for want of a better phrase.

Understanding grief is part of the process of dealing with it, and admittedly, everyone grieves in a different way but there are similarities.

Bereavement support is yet more than that though; it also helps with the practicalities – I had absolutely no idea what to do after Nic passed, it was really only through family and friends that had been through it that I knew what had to be done legally, where to go, who to contact; for all I was concerned, I'd have walked out of the hospital and that would have been that.

We should also think that bereavement support isn't necessarily triggered only after death; the support will start once you're ready for it, including preparing you for what is going to happen. I remember Nic trying to have that conversation with me a few weeks before she died, it wasn't something that I could face up to, or at least not with her. Talking to a professional about it made the situation clearer and possibly a little easier; discussing Nic's death with Nic was not something I was ready for, the very thought of it destroyed me, but having that opportunity with someone that I wasn't that close to (despite them being full of compassion, understanding and friendliness) was an easier way.

Tyler's Perspective

For this next chapter, I thought we'd have something a little different. You've read the stories of other fathers going through some pretty bad times, the general consensus is that yes, it's poo, but you do get through it.

But what about the story from the perspective of the kids that have gone through the mill as well? Do they feel the same?

This next bit is written entirely by Tyler, my 11-year-old son. Aside from some very minor editing, these are his words and his thoughts on the situation. I have to be honest, when I first read it, I was crying like a child who'd had his favourite toy taken away.

"When I was 3, my mum died and me being 11 now, I have to say it's been difficult and now that my dad and aunty Helen are starting a business about it, I kind of feel better about it but I still feel a bit lonely about it because in school and stuff like my friends have both of their parents and when they talk about them I feel a bit weird and different.

My dad's and aunty Helen's business is helping and I think it will be a massive success and I think it's a great idea.

But throughout all of this I made a ton of friends online and it's good to have friends that are like you and are different like you, it's great I think, being able to meet people like you online and be able to play on different games together.

Also in the years between me being 3-11 I have moved houses a lot so it's been difficult to kind of settle anywhere but I do think that this has affected me in good and bad ways.

And I know that one great ways I've managed to have fun is playing video games with my uncle Phil and just plain messing around with him, it's been a great way to forget about everything and just have fun.

And another way to relax is to make thing out of wood and stuff with my grandad, I remember when I made a plane (it didn't fly) but it looked cool.

I've also learned how to turn wood with my grampy, I made a big wooden lamp once.

Growing up without a mum has been weird, I sort of like it because me and dad are really close, but I sometimes wish mum was still here, although I can't really remember her, only from what people tell me and pictures I see of her and me".

Tyler knows that talking about his mum has never been a taboo subject, we've always been very open about it, even in the most difficult times, if he had a question, I would do my best to answer it.

It has taken a number of years to get him settled, I realise that my need to be with someone (anyone!) didn't help, I knew that before I read what he wrote, but finally, he seems happy and settled, he is doing great at school (we're getting so many letters and certificates back from school, we could paper his room).

The recent move to senior school has been something that has helped; he's being challenged academically and the best part is, no one at the school knows his situation, aside from his friends.

Without doubt, losing his mother at such an early age affected him, but you'd never know it now.

Hospice at Home

T he Hospice at Home service is offered by most hospices, and it really is as the name suggests, a hospice environment at home.

The service is designed to bring together the skills and experience of a hospice to the community based end of life care program in a person's own home. This can have a huge benefit for the patient and their family, and could be considered as under the umbrella of palliative care; if a patient is more comfortable or has the wish to be at home when the time comes, this service enables that to happen.

There is of course a great deal of collaboration with other services, be that a community nurse or GP at the local practice; this type of service can stand or fall on the strength of communication.

Having said that, as an independent service provider, the hospice doesn't have the usual politics that could otherwise encumber them; it isn't down to the local council to agree payment or pick up the bill for such a service.

Not all hospices can provide a Hospice at Home service, but there is a national body that represents them: The National Association for Hospice at Home. If there is information needed regarding the service, contact them to ask those questions.

Other Services

Counselling

F orget the Americanised version of being in 'therapy', put aside any notion of being stigmatised; counselling can be one of the greatest sources of comfort and relief that you can receive when things get tough.

While we're putting stereotypes to rest, let's do some more; a counsellor specialises in certain areas, if you're seeing a grief counsellor, you won't be discussing that day when you were three years old and your parent shouted at you and "how that made you feel".

Perhaps I am guilty of stereotyping, but from researching the book, when I mention the topic of counselling, I have generally received two responses:

"Fantastic, couldn't have done without it" or "I'm not discussing my childhood with a stranger".

I suspect that before I had counselling, I had similar feelings and this is something that needs addressing by service providers, it was only through discussing just what counselling meant with my local hospice that I could make an informed choice as to whether I wanted it or not.

I wasn't sure what to expect, my knowledge of counselling had been instilled from years of hearing about Americans being in therapy (sorry – there I go again with the stereotyping); I was sure that I was going to enter a room with a large black settee / sofa / couch (delete as appropriate) to be faced by a stern looking bespectacled woman with a notepad and a man-size box of tissues.

I was half right.

Gaynor didn't wear glasses, there wasn't a sofa, but there was a man-size box of tissues. And tea. Lots of tea.

I remember being surprised at just how little we actually talked about Nic, I really was waiting for the "How did you feel when Nic died?" question but it never came. In fact, I was prepared for it – I had already rehearsed my answer, how could she deny me that?

We spoke about anything and everything, I was waiting for her to start the session before realising that we were actually in the middle of it, but I guess that is part of the skill of a great counsellor.

Gaynor just chatted with me, I didn't recognise a structure but there must have been one, she steered the conversation exactly where she needed it to go, although I have no doubt that she'd say the opposite – it went where I *needed* it to go.

There was no magic bullet answer, it didn't cure me of my grief but it did give me an altogether better outlook on the situation and it was a highlight of my week; I genuinely looked forward to my sessions with Gaynor.

So why should you consider counselling?

It's a great space to gain a better understanding of what's happening in your life, to talk through any fears or concerns that you may have, to give a voice to those thoughts that you just know would upset your family – the reasons are numerous but are tied together with a common theme – communication.

Education and Training

Whether it is from a patient or carer perspective, understanding care or treatment needs is crucial to alleviating some of the anxiety, stress or perhaps fear of being ill enough to warrant a hospice intervention.

In my own experience, I had to learn very quickly the best ways to do things and what I needed to do to not only look after Nic, but myself as well. My mind was absolutely over-loaded with things that I needed to think about, stuff that I *thought* I should be thinking about and then the lesser day-to-day items that life brings on.

What was priority? What would happen if I didn't do X? How should I do Y?

Perhaps it gets back to feeling like you're actually someone that the hospice knows, rather than just being another patient that the over-stressed NHS *has* to deal with.

Again, I cannot stress enough that I believe that NHS and all that it encompasses do an absolutely fantastic job; it isn't from a lack of caring or compassion that you get made to feel you're just on a conveyor, it's purely financial, and no matter who is in No. 10, that doesn't change.

If there are elements of the care that you're not sure of, the hospice will always take the time to explain what it is or the reasoning behind it, they are happy to impart their knowledge to make your life … easier sounds a little crass, given the circumstance, but to help you get through the experience in the best way possible.

The End

As we can see, a hospice is so much more than a final destination for people with a life limiting illness.

One of my hopes for this book is to clear up some of the myths surrounding hospice care and what it involves, I have to be honest, if I'd have known just what a hospice can do when Nic was ill, I'd have made more of an effort to get her into one, rather than waiting for them to contact us.

It's worth noting that while most hospices do receive *some* government funding, the majority are self-financing, ran as a charity and they need to find around 85% of their own money to be sustainable.

I find that an incredible statement.

Surely, organisations such as hospices that provide an absolutely vital service should be protected by state funding (and this is in no way a political statement).

It's really only after talking to Elizabeth Hancock from The Mary Ann Evans Hospice that I began to understand just what proportion of funding most hospices need to find to remain viable. Perhaps next time you're out in the shops and you see someone collecting for a hospice, you'll understand just how vital that money is, and how that any money donated really does get put to good use.

When we first started looking to do something in Nic's memory, we weren't all that sure where to start, never mind if we'd actually do something for the benefit of others.

Initially, we thought of just trying to help other fathers – people that found themselves in the situation that I was in, but as we started looking at what could be done, we realised that there are hundreds of thousands of people that need help, it wasn't our place to distinguish between them.

Back then, I was still in a heck of a mess; I was unable to talk to anyone that I didn't know, my phone was never off divert, I doubted my ability to make a useful contribution to anything that we decided to do.

I've had some fantastic support over the years, and while I can't say that I'm 'fixed', I can definitely say that I've seen the worst of it off.

The idea behind this book was to promote hospices in general and of course, Nic's Legacy, after all, if we can't get support, we can't help people and that is our driving goal.

With some great support from organisations such as Coventry University, in particular Coventry University Social Enterprise and Keith Jeffrey, we have secured funding for the book from the National Lottery 'Awards for All', the Soroptimist International of Rugby Charitable Trust, the Albert Hunt Trust, the Reuben Foundation and Lillie C Johnson, this meant that we can publish the book and distribute it freely to a large number of hospices.

Of course, we would have to say that if you've paid your hard earned money for the book, we appreciate your support and please be safe in the knowledge that the money will be used for a good cause; all profits from the book go toward supporting our cause and therefore, supporting people that really need some help.

All of this has only really been possible due to one person, Nicola Rogers.

It's eight and half years after her death, I still miss her and still think of her.

She was the life and soul of a party, really happy and had the most wonderful smile – pretty much the complete opposite of me!

If you'd like to find out more about what we're doing in Nic's memory, please have a look at our website; www.nicslegacy.org

Of course, if you've read this book and wish to help us along, we're always open to meeting up with new friends to discuss any options that are open to us.

Finally, a bit of shameful stealing of space as I thank those that have got me through this and helped us get where we are:

Mum & Dad (Rogers and Brown), Helen, Phil B, Paul & Amanda, Arff R, Hilary H, Elizabeth H, Mike G, Mike C, John N, Michael M, Bev P, Kay G, Gill H, Maria J and a special mention to the late David Williamson who really made me feel that I could do this.

Thank you all for your love and support.

Jamie

If you'd like to find out more about hospices and the excellent work that they do, have a look at https://www.hospiceuk.org/